Heart's Core

poems by

Joann Gardner

Finishing Line Press
Georgetown, Kentucky

Heart's Core

Copyright © 2023 by Joann Gardner
ISBN 979-8-88838-183-0 First Edition
All rights reserved under International and Pan-American Copyright Conventions. No part of this book may be reproduced in any manner whatsoever without written permission from the publisher, except in the case of brief quotations embodied in critical articles and reviews.

Publisher: Leah Huete de Maines
Editor: Christen Kincaid
Cover Art: Lloyd Baldwin
Author Photo: Carol Gardner
Cover Design: Elizabeth Maines McCleavy

Order online: www.finishinglinepress.com
also available on amazon.com

Author inquiries and mail orders:
Finishing Line Press
P. O. Box 1626
Georgetown, Kentucky 40324
U. S. A.

Table of Contents

Cosam's Journey 1

Setting Out:
    Chipola River 5
    Sarah Evelina 6
    Cosam's Cigar 8
    Arabella in Covington 10
    New Orleans 13
    Concerning Endings 16
    Ghost Orchard 17

Transitional:
    Interlude: His House 21
    A Rocket 22
    Mt. Pisgah 24
    James Brown 25
    Music 27
    Driving North with the Angel of Death 28
    The Last Afternoon of My Father as Himself 32
    Phoenix 33
    Acupuncture 35
    Mowing 37
    Refuge 38
    Gargoyle 40

Coming Home:
    Cats 43
    Maine in Winter 45
    Norway 47
    Crazy Woman 48
    Sturm und Drang 49
    Island Life 50
    Triptych 52
    Nikko Shrine 55
    Awake at Midnight 58

Coda:
    Yin Time 63
    Cosam Rocking 65

The naming of the world, which is an act of creation and re-creation, is not possible if not infused with love.
—*Paulo Freire*

In memory of my parents
Kenneth F. Gardner
and
Mary B. Gardner

With sincere thanks
to those who have believed in my writing
and have helped support it

Cosam's Journey

River of pain, carrying the dead branches of spring, snagged on a rock
on a heart, on a moment of maybe. He leaned over the gunwale, moving
south into a tropical wilderness looking for relief—for a reason
to continue—life, assuage me.

Stare into brown water. Consider a future, personal or otherwise, a word
to remember or forget. Eel grass, the graves of other steamers; wooden
heart, dredge it up. The slow work of barges and cranes, the canal sound

of chains moving through a winch. Grinding cotton, stacked to the beams
of warehouses, wide oak, airy commerce, canvas-bound and caked.

How he awoke to a silence, layer of fog hanging low on the water. Then
in the distance, the sound of an engine cranking. Dead battery, no start
and, then, from the other direction, another engine, trying to spark. Alligators

calling out in the blank, their fiery eyes and slow desires suspended
in the wet muck.

Setting Out

Chipola River

The map offers names like Greenwood and Two Egg, hollow dots to mark
a turn in the road, a sudden collection of buildings. But we have left
that world behind, moving south to a fissure of earth

where the river disappears into the multiple caverns and underground
streams of the Florida aquifer.

                                         We glide now past the ruins of a bridge
marking the entrance to an old plantation, then into an open pool where
multiple clear springs bubble up.

                                         A red clay bank rises to the east of us,
and to the west, water penetrates, forming numerous false passages.

We push back branches, test the give of limbs. Waterlogged palms bend;
cypresses rise from the flooded plain. It is quiet here, except for the pluck
of paddle, the drip of water that rides the curve and falls.

We do not speak, but apply ourselves to the task—you, hung over from
a yesterday of celebrating; me, still wondering what it's all about.

I watch you lift and plant the paddle, deep into a tangle of weeds, feel
my body go from hot to cold, open my eyes to see a swirl of legs,

my back pack, shoes and sunglasses waltzing to the bottom. Above me,
the canoe rocks, cupped, and further on, our cooler bobs away from us,
downstream.

                  A fat alligator hunkers on the bank—knees cocked,
considering. "Are you all right?" you ask. "Fine," I mutter, as I struggle
toward the shore. We recapture what we can of our belongings,

upturn the sad canoe. We stand there shivering on an island of weeds:
deep in the Florida wilderness, with only one paddle, and no clear sense
of where to go.

Sarah Evelina

A woman's word has no currency here…that's what
they said   assuming authority   the way they do
in this and every contest   as if we had no brain
to speak of   no thought that counted   the affairs
of men inscrutable   or so they'd have us think.

Are those words whispered to her husband in bed
not valuable?   the reproof she gave to the boy
all flush with certainty   a child of two and headstrong?
Women are   after all   in charge of the household
so how could they not have something to say
and would it be too much   she wonders   for him
to listen and to trust?

        Not to show up in the papers
she knows   family matters   so-and-so files for divorce
husband warns shopkeepers   not to extend credit
to estranged wife   apparently bent on spending
haphazardly   unfit mother   but there are others

    whose story is not told

what of them?

      *

A bird explores the cracks in the fence   she writes
a letter home   dips pen in ink   scratches   clock
ticks   slow continuance   mending stocking   taking
stock

sometimes I think of the ways I spend my time
the words that accompany me   the choices
I've made   working my way into his life   a promise
not to abandon promises   settling here at a distance
from family and friends   Do not marry this
Christian man   they told me   and I   I willfully
did otherwise

*

mended his jacket the other day torn at
the shoulder   and his cravat worn from years
of tying   in the same place always   he thinks
too much writes with expectation

of being heard   trying to find in the physical
application of ink and type   letters pressed
to the page   what makes for communication

but he returns to me at night a spent child
and only I know what shakes him weak like
a rag   his hollow cough from too much thinking

closed rooms   fumes   buckets of waste
the inexplicable   need to be heard   my need
to be near and hear him   and also   yes   to speak

Cosam's Cigar

You keep me humble   bold cigar   teaching me lessons
beyond the preacher's skill   When I am here alone

with you   after the printers have gone home   the paper
put to sleep   I weave a sinuous trail of smoke up beyond

the rafters   And then   because the Muse is near
            compose some stumbling lines:

*

Like you   the hero burns   then turns to ashes   mingles
with the dust   When your feathery column grows

and loses its vital spark   I trace how mighty realms
once rose like that and fell   And when my broken

lungs fill up   a silence softens all   I wonder about
the clutch of death   how it will come to me

no more ink-black struggles   no more thinking
what this friend thinks   or this ambitious man

no more brooding on my own violence   the things
I've done   my self a stranger

We burn like this   you and I   from the inside out
consume   I only know   that night it seemed a simple

thing to do   light the match   take one slow pull
before placing you   your smoldering tip   near the keg

of gunpowder   tell the rowdies bent on hanging me
one more step   and we will all go to hell together.

That's what I said   together   and liking their own
lives   more than their convictions   they left
stumbling to get out the door.

*

And   now   I strike that match again   breathe in your
slow convictions   and as I do   compose these lines

an ode for tomorrow's paper   since literature
advances the cause of civilization   and I am
by your methods amply schooled:

Poor and rich alike, all the sweet
Works of nature die
And what am I this moment
But a little snowy heap
That soon must sleep in ashes
Bow to dust?

When I see your smoke roil high
Your ashes fall away
I know that thus my soul will fly
As it leaves my body to decay…

Arabella in Covington

At Pensacola, the rain subsides. Out on the Gulf,
the sun draws water. I pass a truck pulling cattle.

The countryside whizzes past. These wooly breathers,
wide-eyed, sniffing.

Exit at Spanish Fort, find oyster houses down
along the flats. Steam from kitchens rises: rickety
houses, salt-saturated wood.

I drive west into Mississippi; names like Pascagoula
and Biloxi rise like bubbles of sound. On past

Hattiesburg and Gulfport, listening to Christmas
Carols on the radio, the season of birth, the darkest
time of the year.

*

Crossing over into St. Tammany Parish: Pearl River
sparkling, pale moss in trees. A sign with a steamboat
announces, "Louisiana Welcomes You."

*

Standing in the Covington Cemetery, ground spongy
from continuous rain: a series of carriage houses,

as from a back alley viewed: crumbling monuments,
cracked pots, lichen, moisture, concrete drains.

Two stones enclosed by an ironwork fence: the first,
of the man, vital statistics intact; the second,

of the woman, stating only "Our Mother."
Numerous other graves around them bending in.

Standing here on this blustery day, as if I'd just
come home to something. A silence reaching back.

And only I know who this woman was and why
she was important beyond the inscription here.

*

I drive south across Lake Pontchartrain, everything
thawing out from last night's frost. Occasionally,

a channel marker or buoy appears. Otherwise,
a deserted expanse of pale color hovers.

A police car speeds by. Momentary panic as traffic
clears a space, then resumes its steady pulse.

White and black water birds converge on the surface.
A pelican lumbers overhead, its brown wings aching.

Causeway stretches upward, then sinks into the froth.
Enigmatic pylons; then, the high rises of the city,
poised on a lip of land.

*

Cigar box houses made of wood. Aluminum and hard
plastic awnings imitate the stiff drape of cloth.

Cemeteries crouch behind stuccoed walls. Filagreed
bungalows, turquoise, yellow, white.

*

In the Louisiana Room of the Tulane Library, I rediscover
the City Directory, the names and addresses of those

whose stories I am piecing, their occupations, year
to year. Sarah Evelina, Cosam Julian, Frank and Napier.

Even E. R. Randolph, the homeopathic doctor, his office
on Robin Street. Big luxury cars block the narrow path.

Valets rip backwards down the road near Commander's.
Elegant ladies and smartly dressed men proceed
to the door.

I have lunch on the levee at Audubon Park, where once
we sat in springtime, our bicycles and backpacks
abandoned on the lawn

*

Lake Pontchartrain is becalmed. A silvery flatness,
mother of pearl; the horizon, blue-gray, and, above it,
a blue-bland sky.

I take the back route to Baton Rouge through a series
of small towns, foot-dragging traffic, substations,
electric wires.

The approach to the city, an endless array of concrete,
plastic and tin facades, directions that disappear down

back alleyways, come to a halt at the river, and a library
no more helpful or informed than the listless teenager

who eyes me from the stoop. Return to the interstate
at high point of rush hour, traffic slowed to a crawl.

Louisiana drivers and their custom trucks, Buick
Skylarks and sparkly Cadillacs with brougham tops.

They follow close, pass fast, cut in. Interiors masked
by tinted windows. Ride the clutch, hit the brakes,

grind the teeth. Starlight. Barreling fast into the East.
I look up into a full moon rising.

New Orleans

A giant cockroach appears at sunset from the depths of the air conditioner, which, held together by wads of sticky duct tape, drips and groans.

Said cockroach is fat and black. Very sexy, you know, and is willing to engage in conversation, if only you would give him a chance.

He harbors a mistress who stays behind, in the coils of dust and cool, closer to the margins, the *je ne sais quoi* of trash compactors.

He wiggles his antennae.—Food for Monsieur who has to eat? Or his attractive lady, still waiting in the wings? What say? *Manger?*

I go at him with a shoe, but he is agile. Retreats into the coils.—That is not, what you say, very friendly for one so new arrived. I stop, lean back,

eye the food on the sill that will rot before morning.—Okay, Monsieur, have at it, but try to be discreet.

*

The brass bell of the St. Charles trolley rings. Gears crank, engine gets under way. A passenger buzzes for his stop, pulling once

on the slack gray cord that's strung above the windows. Screech of metal brakes, doors open, slap shut. Ring-ring.

*

This is a place of contrasts, of cool breezes up from the river, of hot days, magnolias, Zydeco, sweat. Expansive porches and floor-

length windows, with rarely a curtain to obstruct. I gaze back into the spaces of a house, to cherry sideboards, ornate moldings,

pristine white walls. Next door, a door of intricately cut glass, light refracting from a thousand brilliant surfaces.

*

Filth litters sidewalks. The smell of rotting food. In the Quarter, you can
buy a daiquiri or a beer and roam the sidewalks, working on a buzz.

A couple of old drunks, their hair matted, slur and tease each other
about that woman over there, the prospects.

We are on Bourbon Street, after all, where you can get anything
you want by way of excess, where windows and doors open

to reveal a taste of rose-colored darkness. Music, good and awful,
penetrates the street.

*

And this is what he came to, this young lawyer from the North,
hung out his shingle, advertised in the press, served in local

government, absorbed punishment for his sins; buried at last
at Métarie, where thoroughbreds once ran.

A note in the *Crescent*
      confirms his presence here:

           T. A. Bartlette, Attorney at Law,
               tenders his services to all,

           assuring his clients that matters
               entrusted to his care

           will be faithfully attended to…

*

Garbage Eaters in their Jesus sandals and blue raincoats push
their bikes down to the Market, scavenging for food. The bruised

and redolent, they place carefully in a cardboard box attached
to the back of their bicycles, then push back across Jackson Square.

I stop in for coffee at Marie's, the smell of chicory, steam rising,
warm pastry (beignets). Through the window, a current of humanity

passes: vendors peddle plastic beads, boys with bottle caps attached
to sneakers tap for tourists eagerly and the silver-painted man

on his pedestal stands stock-still, unheeding

*

A small rain saturates my clothes. The papers in my satchel bleed,
turn slowly to mush. On Canal Street, people cluster under awnings,

crowd the entrances to shops. Sometimes, scaffolding,
a covered walkway under which to proceed.

In the library, I unpack papers and books, cast soaked umbrella
to the floor, sit in damp clothes examining indexes, manuscripts.

Gaze into a luminous box. Pale shadows of words rising
from a white screen.

Concerning Endings

An old woman in her bedroom slippers
positions herself in the street.

She pounds a battered keyboard
and sings the blues, as if she knew
what she was talking about.

In her pillbox hat, white flowered
dress and multi-colored scarf,
remembering:

All this vibrant city under siege;
houses flooded; people on their roofs
straining to survive

When the water rise, it take
our lives away,
our dreams and our lives,
when the water rise…

Ghost Orchid

Pale green starfish tentacles weave themselves into the rough
bark of trees: live oak, cypress, in the swamp beyond the reaches
of human experience.

Once a year, it blooms pure white in this tangle of palm trees—
vines, mold, slime, lizards—blooms, embedded in bark, yet
seemingly free of attachments.

Dark dream of pools, cool petals spreading, elegant tails unfurl
like cream from a pitcher at dusk beneath the hardwood canopy.

Undetected, except for the bee, who wanders sluggishly
plant to plant, or the giant sphinx, whose cumbrous body lands
on a soft lip and stares into that pale face staring back.

One of a set who knows the ache of beauty, simple, singular
and the delicate scent of love blossoming in unlikely places.

Transitional

Interlude: His House

A basket of mung beans putting forth shoots,
breathing on their own in the locked container.

Ripe tomatoes on a sill, hefty, firm, and the knife
slices through them like paper.

An old bicycle in the hall, disassembled, dusty,
tires flat, rims rusty.

Lifting a bicycle over the stile on a path
after someone you've believed in, something you need,

like sunshine, like green, trying to get down to business.
As if a voice would call, as if anyone could hear it.

Put a finger on it, the words that warm: he or she
returning over the sea to the deaf island.

A Rocket

A concrete
truck pulls out
onto the roadway
pauses to adjust itself
cranks gears then slow-
wheeling labors uphill
toward the light

*

early evening
sunlight dazzles
red clay of earth
exhaust pipe
churning   barrel
pulses   engine swirls

*

the barbed wire
across the road sparkles
and sings behind it
field mice   run for cover
amid stiff straw

*

"I spend days and days
being neither happy nor sad,"
she tells me,
the sound of her voice   beyond
the static bounce

*

As for the stars
they are mementoes
crushed tinsel from a Christmas
at the beach when everyone
was happy and alive

how the hard wire
is wound into
boughs
that catch on branches

disintegrate
into tinseled sparks that
follow me out the door

*

like the ladybug
that followed me
home that November
alive to the prospect
of a winter without
snow

Mt. Pisgah

She spills out of her car into the ponderous darkness,
fog settling fast on Pisgah Mountain. That bears can be
unpredictable rises from a shimmering surface of sign.

Perhaps at night or at dawn, they will lumber into the clearing,
sniff at the perimeter, nudge this silent hulk. ...A bird,
half in sleep, calls out, "Are you there?" A breathlessness,
a pause, then the monotonous chirping starts again.

Stars burn through a basket of clouds, travel the distance
required of them: fuzzy, indistinct, then clear, and one
fast-moving planet, perhaps the spaceship Mir,
looks down from its isolated weightlessness in the sky.

She climbs back into her car, adjusts her body around
suitcases and coolers. Listens hard for human sounds,
searches the distance for a light.

It rains on and off. Moisture gathers in the grass.
Her feet get cold and warm again. She wakes and sleeps
and dreams she is a bear. And it is winter in her dreams,
as she settles down into the leaves at the mouth of the cave.

Turning to the wall, she scents the moisture, reaching
back through stone and darkness underground.
Turning again, she encounters absence: a brittle wind,
her own pitted growl.

Next morning, a falcon in a tree calls out. She catches
in her nostrils the sandy sweetness of the mountain laurel
as she moves up the path, wanting water to splash on her face.

How many nights like this would turn her into a derelict?
She estimates only one.

James Brown

An explosion of sound as searchlights pan the stage.
A man in white, big hair slicked, saunters out to introduce:
The Generals of Soul. A band in fuchsia zoot suits plays
electric, wild. Then, three swaying backup singers in gowns.
Lights left. *"Ladies and Gentlemen, The Bittersweets."*
We applaud. Two of an original three go-go dancers
work their legs up and down, but the man we've all been
waiting for, the Amazing Mr. Funk, where is he? We crane
our necks, search the stage, breathless wait, but do not see.
Then, with Supreme Dignity, the Godfather of Soul struts out,
fresh from his unwanted vacation—his unfortunate
incarceration—hair coifed, unmovable, unmoved.

In green taffeta and gold glitter, black pointy boots shuffling,
he gives us what we want, a familiar "Turn It Loose."
Off comes the cape and two sets of drums, two trumpets,
two saxes, two guitars, one piano, three back-up singers,
two go-go girls, one announcer and the one and only
James Brown get down.

He throws mike, dips, catches it, sweats, "Like a Sex Machine."
"Mama, Mama, Mama," raw rock and we remember.
James Brown from Georgia picking it up where he left off.
"I was born dead with a caul over my face. They revived me,
and I started singing, "Please, Please, Please." My mother
quit school in the fourth grade, my father in the second.
I made it to the seventh." ("Papa Got a Brand New Bag.")
"Hey, let's have a hand for John Paul II. I'm a Baptist myself.
Do you believe?" "And let's have thirty seconds of silence,
please, for King Assad of Syria, who wanted peace—and for
Menachim Begin and Martin Luther King, and John F. Kennedy,
and Robert Kennedy." "We got to stop the violence. It makes
me wanna scream."

More dancing, swinging, rock, feet pounding. And then some
sweet stuff with the girls: they dance together like two spoons
or waltz in a circle smiling. He asks his lead guitar man,

"You ever seen B.B. King?" And the answer comes back
as music, yes. "You ever hear him play Lucile?" Yes, Lucile,
straining at the chords. "What you say your guitar was named—
Matilda? Well, play Matilda like you'd play her up against
B.B. King." Down on his knees, making his guitar plead, sing.

"It's a man's world," and the men in the audience cheer.
"It's a man's world, but it wouldn't mean nothin, no, it wouldn't
mean nothin, without a woman or a girl."

The phenomenal James steps back, outa gas, staggers a few feet,
stage front, slumps, weeping. Announcer comes, puts cape on
shoulders. He gets up, throws it off, returns to the mike and screams,
"It wouldn't mean nothin' without a woman or a girl."

The process is repeated, death, renewal, surge, and the music,
yes, the music reaching, deep into this star-strewn evening:
"Ladies and gentlemen, James Brown,

> *James Brown,*
> *James Brown.*

Music

We sit in pews, straight-backed, while around us,
men in fuchsia tights, women in horned hats,
put themselves through the musical calisthenics
of fifteenth-century Germany. A discipline that
gets beyond itself, medieval instruments having
minds of their own.

"Each conductor," says the author, "must perform
these pieces as best he can." So, here are sackbuts
sawing, dulcians making sweet, violas and voices
trying to tune; rackets making their tiresome racket,
crumhorns crunching notes.

Everyone sweats. The man in the pew behind me
convulses and spits. I sit like the sphinx absorbing
this experience, while Solveig the Soprano stands
board-straight in the balcony, belting out her misery
("I am weary from moaning; every night I flood
my bed with tears.").

And I, sufficiently tranquilized by multiple
mood-warming medications, no longer rehearse
words of reproach, but wonder about my future
and curse my enemies as Solveig does—not with
a pain that penetrates my heart, not with a heart
or a conviction—but with a small blue glow that
is cool at the center as the isinglass on the church
windows, as elegant as the recorder's
ad libitum curls.

Jubilate Des. Where does the pain go, the weight
that sits on the brow and heart? Does it sit hovering,
waiting to descend again, or has it left with my
convictions, the sudden sense that I cannot
change the world?

Sackbuts, chronetti, dulcians, lutes. I am on my knees
in my sister's sub-basement, murmuring, *Lift me up,
 O Lord...* to my actual feet, to an actual belief that
we are wise in our laughter, not grim with the knitted

brow, but patiently confident that it all works out,
like this melody that stretches into painful continua,
but comes down solid at the end.

Driving North with the Angel of Death

He sits beside me   pistol on his lap   stale
tobacco breath   stains on his teeth   Don't
know how I got stuck with this problem
hanging out in front of the convenience
store rest room   something about how he
must get up North to see someone   Clearly
a fabrication   He has no friends here

He puts his boots up on the dashboard
spins the cylinder of his gun   an old
Russian model   roulette-click   laughs
loudly at some sick   joke he's made
spurs digging deep into naugahide

Out of the corner of one eye, I note his
nervous tick   making for unpredictable
conclusions   He finds the muzzle cold.
"It's cold"   he says   then presses it
to my cheek   "Yes"   I say and realize
that if he pulls the trigger now   my
molars will explode   blowing a hole
big enough to gaze through

"Cheap dentistry"   he concludes   and
laughs again   as if it were the funniest
thing in the world   I don't care by now
I don't   which is not to say   I'm having
fun or he's   the answer to my dreams
but that   after a point   one stops resisting
and anyway   I brought it on myself

He rolls the window down   Soon   he's
up on the passenger seat   fiddling with
his pants   I want to say   cut it out   get
down   but he's trying to piss out the
window   "What a gas"   he says and spits
a foam-flecked wad drips leisurely
down the door.

Outside   it's raining   slicking the gray
road black   so I turn on the radio   It's
playing Strauss   which I think might

calm him   or else   make him really angry.
Either way   push through to another intensity
and much to my surprise   he seems to like it
moving his hand with a brown-bagged
Jax bottle as if conducting an orchestra

He's taken with the performance   or so
he tells me   tapping into his feminine side
which he'd suppressed long ago   because
his mother used to beat him   senseless
through lack of love   and where is that
goddamned cigarette lighter anyway?

He slams the bottle down   splintering
the glass   It goes everywhere   the frothy
brew   the spiky shards   the blood-soaked
bag   which he tries to stuff into my mouth,
distracting me   as he grabs the wheel   and
turns it   hard right   Instinctively   I turn
back   The car begins to tip   first one way
then the other   like an unskilled skater
on a frozen pond

until I realize there's no way out   unless I
commit myself to the movement   Strauss
playing dreamily   I turn into the skid
pirouette through traffic   Everything
slows   down   I smell the acrid sizzle of my tires
see the sea of cars   ahead of me blazing   red alarm
await impact   like a pinball   falling aimlessly
through space   a maze of bumpers   helpless
except   suddenly we come to rest

backwards on a small V of grass   facing
traffic   steam rising   engine stalled and silent
Cars zip around us   making for their usual

destinations   He opens the door   gets out
leans back into the window   where I sit
pinned   to my seat breathing   "Just kidding"
he says   and is gone.

The Last Afternoon of My Father as Himself

In the light rain, he watched, wordless as I worked,
although pleading with his eyes for me to stop.

Mosquitoes thick as hacksaws, and he without
the strength or the will to swat them.

Earlier, at the airport, he had walked behind: pallor
on his face, stumbling gait, halting conversation.

Much sleeping, far too much sleeping, then a day
and a night when it all fell apart, the last afternoon
of my father as himself.

*

"I feel like I'm in a box," he said. "You sleep." Then,
a flashlight in my eyes, antic pacing. "No kidding,
Get help."

I drive to the local motel, the only telephone
on the island. It's 3 A.M., and I'm shoving quarters
into a slot, trying to find answers.

I can't shake the agony of that moment, the simple
fact of my inadequacy: what life asks of you or death,

how those who haven't experienced it know nothing,
and those who show no sympathy are lost.

Phoenix

Disconnected phone numbers, information booths that have no
information, white pager phones that echo in the din my own

name back at me, but no sense of other than mockery identity,
shadow purpose, lightness, carrying on. What should have been

is not. Some faces friendly, some desperate; all strangers,
as we move along the moving walkway, the dizzying crush

from sleeplessness, like angels on a screen. But the burden
of baggage seems real enough and cannot be ignored, so it is

lugged from phone to curbside and back again to phone.
I hesitate in front of an illumined board. A man approaches,

asks me where I'm going. When I cannot answer, he turns
on his heel and leaves. So, I sit in a chair next to a pregnant

woman and her young daughter, who also wait for no one
in particular. The girl plays patty-cake, sings a familiar song,

with strange new words—"Mommy's little baby has HIV—
which makes the mother laugh. And I imagine we are on this

journey together, to the bean field to pick beans, and we
are waiting for the bus to take us down that dusty road…

*

This young Charon pedals his cab slowly, speaks soothingly
of this desert place, while outside, spiny cacti push up through

sand and dirt. A gouged-out riverbed inches its way through
traffic, tingle of automotive life, a sense that someone knows

where they are going if not me. So, I sit in the diner, at the counter,
on a stool—a rattle of plates and voices, the waitress carrying on—

just sit there, before a picture, in a diner, of James Dean. "Oh,
I didn't see you," the waitress exclaims at last. And, after a night

at the Day's Inn, I pick up this notebook: it's last year's words,
reporting last year's language, and the poem is gone, the one

that was going to save me. So much for sacred journeys
and relying on the self. I remember the face of that woman

lost on the train to York, desperate to reach a station not
on any map. The lit windows of the cars as the engine

pulls out for the yard, the panic-stricken figure pressing
fingers against the glass. Swiftly, an amnesia in which

the pieces fall apart, then are reassembled, except that you
are factored out—your needs, your expectations, your senses,

your very self. I call a friend up at midnight to ask if he's
all right. "Sure," he says, "are you?"

Acupuncture

The most important thing is for you to be nice people.
                                          —The 14th Dalai Lama

Like, today, I am surly, and I don't know why, except
I don't believe she's interested, and why, for heaven's sake,
did she bring it up if she was not going to address it.
There are other conversations that fit in better with the blank
ceiling, the pocked wall, the one-eyed ozonator that blows
its *Om* into the room. The previous patient, for instance,
what was wrong with her, or who was the woman
in the office next door—the portly one with the wicker purse,
or her client who arrived late and ate her lunch in the waiting room.
"You shouldn't hurry," I chided her. "I'm starving," she replied.

So, what she says surprises me, coming as it does, on the heels
of this event.—It's not so much that I haven't "been through a lot,"
as she informs me, but that she feels compelled to put it into words.
I want her to take it back, to take it on, to take me in her arms,
and let me blubber like a baby 'til I am empty, but she merely
looks at me and waits, half a beat, before pressing on.
Perhaps, she is writing ("Patient reacts") in her big black book.
I resolve to write as well. ("Acupuncturist opens wound.")
—A war of silences, of scratching pens. She asks how long
it's been since the onset of hard times: my father's illness,

the death of colleagues, the unspoken loss of love. I say three
years, but I don't know. Perhaps, it's been forever, perhaps, since
I was born. Later, I discover it's been more like six. Six is long.
It's not forever. It's certainly long enough. I announce if I get sick,
it will be from stress. She looks at me as if I'd turned into a bat
and she needed a bucket to contain me. "Some of it's biology,"
she counters. "If I get sick, I won't beat myself up for not
saying no." (I gather her stress is not saying no—to people who
ask to be fit in because of some imagined emergency or other,
which turns out to be nothing, but an inflated sense of self-worth.)
But this one is not, the one that lies on the table, a white lump

that needs to be told, "You've been through a lot," because,
somehow, she doesn't know, and then cries when told " a lot."
No, this is the real thing, the weak chi, the suffering artist, still
learning how to live, still learning at fifty, and she wants to help,
identifies with the need, and knows that part of the concern
is crazy, the leap her father took into the unknown. She takes
my hand, lifts my wrist, and feels my pulse. Then, goes around
to the other side, lifts the other hand and slides hers into mine,
holds it there, exactly grasping—not acting, not overwhelmed
or overwhelming, but matching warmth to warmth. She looks at me

when she speaks, does not turn away, but presses her fingers into
the veins, gauging the current there, the will. "Your pulse is stronger
than it was. Whatever you're doing, keep it up." When she tells me to,
I sit up, put my legs down over the side. I feel her fingers count
the distance outward from the spine, mark an ex where the moxa
will go. She slips her hand in back of my bra, then, pulls the small
tab up. Pushes down on my shoulder so I'm sitting straight. "Sorry,"
I say. "That's all right," she replies, and applies the smoldering moss.

I am telling her what I've been doing, which consists of crawling
on my belly on the roof of the camp. I want to indicate that I
have no intention of doing it again, but she wants to know more
about this camp—where it is, what it's like, what else I've done.
Made a patio. Cut some trees. "What's the patio made of?"
"Bluestone." "Nice." A flag of energy breezes upward from the spine.
I can't forget the needles in the feet—further up than usual and a little
painful, like nails—and the rest, for which I desired music, and the
subsequent pulse change ("nice") and the follow up, for which she says,
"You'll just call me?" and "Acupuncture is a good preventative;

keeps the body from going wrong." But it's all there, along with my
desire to thank her, to express my deep regard, which I cannot do,
now or ever, because there are no words.

Mowing

Two boys on bicycles pedal up and down the street.
Their crash helmets fall down around their faces.

An old dog gets up from his place on the lawn,
lumbers out to inspect them, lumbers back.

On the boulevard, a large pleasure boat, strapped
to the back of a truck, inches its way through traffic.

I work most of the day, stitching my argument
into terse sentences. Down on the lawn, a man

in faded ball cap maneuvers around rocks, grooming
the green grass on which the retirees gaze.

He turns his huge mower around planted trees,
shifting gears, lowering the steel blade, slicing.

Refuge

A numbered house not identified
externally, a complex of buildings
behind tall fences, the rooms so
silent only traces of habitation,

tennis shoes with socks
in them, a few scattered
plastic toys, TV blaring
no one watching.

"Transitional" means
preparing to move from one
life to another
leaving behind a history
of abuse.

Here are cubbies, locked
each with a modest cache
of toiletries, food,

mementoes from a time
when it didn't happen,
or it happened, but
she believed it would stop.

Why would a woman not
leave her abuser?

She fears he will retaliate.
She loves him. It's against
her religion. She has no-
where to go.

Blue Jay in a live oak singing,
Yippee, Hey-hey, Crank-crank.
Two teen-aged boys on skateboards
roll down the street, pushing
scooter-style, wheels whir.

In the neighborhoods, on street
corners, chatting at the mall, we have
no way of knowing who is

under siege, what fear or
desperation drives them
to seek relief.

You may be a safe person
for someone, she tells me.
(It occurs to me I am).

Gargoyle

This stone face stretches its chin into the ether,
its gray eyes ossified, its cavernous ears in the wind.
Uncertain if it hears or sees, it yearns to be something.

Notice the neck muscles taut, the hollow cheeks
from years of abstinence, the bald head, naked,
the building from which it grows, like a cartoon

bubble trying to liberate itself from the mouth,
the source, grimace, cornice. Notice the sea-blue,
misty horizon stretching like hope, and the distant

possibility that he could shake this senselessness,
this brittle pose, launch himself from this precipice,
free like a bird, dreaming of second chances.

Coming Home

Cats

They sit on junk piles, surveying their realm: scattered paper
towels and cans on the lawn from a trash bag they'd got into.
They look worn: their fur stained black around the face

or dingy from walking through ditches. The Tomcat is close-
cropped, bold. He marches up and down the road. Each season,
he gets to hump whatever's available—which is a lot, although
the gene pool is limited.

The new kittens romp with joy in the sun, not knowing much
about hard times, although living under the porches of these
abandoned houses or in the rain exposed cannot be idyllic.

The orange ones, longhaired and short, are attractive, but too
many replications of the same thing erodes enthusiasm. When
afflicted by malnutrition or pared down by disease, they are
defiant, mean, carrying on without welcome in the world.

A cat is crying, obviously in heat. Soon, another emerges
from the woods and rushes up the hill to the rescue. Last night,
she caterwauled around the base of the houses, desperate
for attention.

The renters took her in, feeding her. Then, she wouldn't leave.
They thought she was pretty, black and gold, but today, when
they went home, they did not take her.

Yesterday, I discovered that one had relieved himself
on the plastic netting covering my garden. A substantial dried
turd stood suspended, several inches from the ground. I shook
it loose, propped up the netting so it was more difficult
to tread on.

My hens and chicks have been deracinated by their scratching.
They cover their scat half-heartedly, deposit it where it will have
the most impact: in front of the mailbox, around the perimeter
of my car, on the path to the house, under the house in huge
petrified piles.

I can't walk without picking it up. Can't do anything without
them getting into it. They lounge in the road, sit atop the neighbor's

traps and junked cars, squat on the porch, nose the screen when
they smell food, run fast when I hurl myself out the door,
foe to cats, defender of territory.

When I get back from town, I do not rest because the cats
have been at work, pooping under the mailbox, soiling the car
cover I've just cleaned. I get out the cat repellant and spray
liberally, everywhere, before settling down for the night,
exhausted.

Maine in Winter

The water in the Gulf of Maine   is deep blue cold
coming in   One lighthouse blinks at another   from across
the sound   Small white needles   of fishing boats
split the surface   leaving a wedge widening behind them

Darkness comes early here   slams the world shut
cars rush home along 295   Lights go on in the houses

"You won't have any trouble there on the island,"
my uncle tells me   "The water temperature is 40 degrees"

"We've had snow   We've had frost   Not enough
to bother with   although it won't stand   much longer
that way"

He tells me about the pump   how water settles
in the chambers   and with a good hard freeze
the metal expands and cracks

I know   I've made a thousand-dollar journey   to save
a two-hundred-fifty-dollar pump

***

I drive past my old high school   and then the middle
school where friends held forth   The place is a-buzz
with activity   but not my activity

I pause on the Boulevard   and gaze across the bay
at the bristling city   see the Old North school   where
my father entered   his elegant letters in lined notebooks

Munjoy Hill and the Observatory   which always
seemed too small to observe much of anything   still
tourists come   climb the spiral stairway   to the top

***

At the island   I inspect the new bathroom   notice
the soft light   streaming through the skylight   squeeze

out the sponge   beneath the hot water spigot   wipe up
moisture on the floor

Workmen have inhabited this space   have used the stove
to warm up their meals   In the living room   are two
quilted pads   covered with sawdust and boot prints
an old paint-splattered radio   its antennae tipped quizzically
to pick up tunes

                    ***

I go up the road to talk to Chris   his son Cyrus   plays
on the floor   and watches TV   We talk about the lobster
industry   the season's catch   summers here on the island

He asks if I'll come here to live   when I retire   or if
I've grown used to life "away"   I gaze out the window
at the bare trees   steel-colored water   churning
There is silence   between us

Norway

A knock on the door invites answers. Outdoors,
click-drift, fishing boats, fiords.

Slice of salmon, dark brew. Elk travel on crisp hooves.
Our favorite flavor, tang.

Flame in the belly. Woolen hands, friendly. The rough
cut, and the gentle steam rising. The secret lip of sea.

Risk everything, long winter nights, the bright
displays, sound heaves on the frozen tundra, water,
Lillehammer.

And, in this country, a message near the door, how one
must make the long retreat alone. Gather up the children,
wrap them in fur, quick as the stars and no notion
of where they would come from, but certain
as the seasons they would come.

Got to flee. Got to get out of here. Got to jump quick.
(Gotcha, Batya.) Take something for the journey:
a book of names, collection of coins, light-growing
lantern, leading us to that jagged shore, wooden
boat, waves pounding.

Let's say we know how it feels, everything forgetting,
words like a curse, or a grumble, cold. They took what
we had, our hopes, our homes. Sobbed with regret,
even before we left the harbor.

Planet waves, seeking a landed miracle. Mother and son,
a distant reminder, warming their hands by the fire.

Let's peel potatoes, break bread, think-sing, sip tea,
loggy-headed, light the lamp. "What do you want
from the old house?" her mother asked. "Not a thing,"
she replied and meant it. "Let's rest, then. Yes,"
on the wooly surface, on goose ticking glad, and they did.

Crazy Woman

Across the street
children work
the ice.

You can hear
the steady crunch
of feet, muffled
breakage.

On the avenue,
the crazy woman
walks, hair
flying—cold
purposeful.

The houses are vacant.
(What kind of news
is that?)

Children work
the ice.

Into and out
of that same
intersection

trying to take
the edge off

this restlessness
this drive.

Sturm und Drang

After much gathering, rain falls. Thunder
ripples like dominoes, collapsing in a line.
The new leaves, drenched green, sag.
The bark of trees, lichen-spotted, darken.
A rush of activity, as drops fall, striking
the inside wall of fireplace,
                                      windows,
doors and eaves, hypnotically dropping.
Caked dirt, a patina of pollen, thickening.
Rivulets, clogging. Cats
crouch beneath leaf cover, squinting,
and the wet drops pummel their fur.
Moss grows, slugs proliferate.
The woods fill up with water. Mosquitoes
hum, hungry for blood, and then, hail
comes, sudden as golf balls, striking walls
and windows. Then, big as baseballs
                                A furious
pounding, as lightning splits the sky.
Brittle sparks, jagged scars,
explosive, riveting, harrowing rain
and the blinding, aching, punishing
thunder, finding me here,
Lear-like, hovering and prone
to my own intensities.
                            Again and again,
light flickers, electric current sizzles,
streaking the screen green, defeating
the lamps. Then, darkness, followed
by the eerie white of lightning through
the window, the disconcerting roar and
retreat, softening, the rain
slow-plinking
drops on fender, on shed roof, steam
rising from pavement. A pillow of mist
in the trees, the hiss of aftermath, before
the birds come out, announcing the all clear.

Island Life

Awakened by the neighbors' dogs to fog hanging in trees. Muggy weather, between hot and cold. Smell the ocean. Hear the hollow bong-bing of the buoy tossed by swells.

At Gisland Farm, I sit in the shelter overlooking the river. A bunch of day campers trots by, asks if I've seen any kids. I say no. Eventually, they wander off.

Mosquitoes kiss the screen. The light is golden, slanted. Grass stretches a rich green over rocks. Slug weather; a silver trail across the lawn.

Mushrooms rise from moss, topple with ripeness. Finally, the wild rose blooms, sends out its delicate runners. Pink blossoms and the new leaves push upward; prickly stocks turn heavy, curl down.

A moth flutters up the wall, feeling with its body for a resting place. The simple spider spins palimpsest on the screen. The ocean keeps up its steady tympanum. The bell waltzes unevenly on its stem.

At dawn, you can hear the hum of diesels. Lobstermen crank up their engines, head out the cove. My neighbor rumbles up the road and stops just beyond the house. Backs up onto the circle, then turns and rolls down the hill again.

Continuing hot-cold restlessness. Tear off clothes. Add blankets. Take blankets off. Suddenly hot.

Feral cats have cleaned out the woods. A lone survivor sings, "hey, birdie; hey, birdie." He's trying to attract a lover, seemingly unaware of the dangers of making himself heard.

And there is a resident squirrel—just one—whose tail shows evidence of repeated alarums. Yesterday, the coon cat cornered him in a tree next to the driveway. Bristling kinetically, eye to eye.

It rains, day in, day out. Slugs stick to doorframe. Fog floats in, hangs in branches. "Hey, birdie; hey, birdie," as darkness descends.

Shush of waves, the subtle hum of engines returning, the slow irregular bong-bing of bell buoy off the back of the island.

Dampness, an uncertain cold, wrapped in a feverish blanket, reading the same soggy paragraph over and over, writing down words, erasing them.

The eerie green light in the living room turns out to be the channel changer for the TV, the green light on my computer. And then the yellow streetlight, golden pale, cutting a swath through trees.

No moon no never moon, because it's overcast. No stars except for once, they set off fireworks on the hill. Roman candles: fizz, whirr, articulate bursts of color spreading in the night sky.

Triptych

i.

If one of these tall pines
should pull itself up
and lunge forward into
the underbrush, should
break a path headlong

into foliage, splinter,
crush and crack in
streams of ripening
sunlight, if one of these

tall pines should fall, its
roots upended suddenly,
the sodden earth still
coming off in clumps,

if one of these tall pines
should fall and there
were no one there to hear
it, no one there who hears,
would it make a sound?

(What's a sound?)

ii.

Mrs. Lewisohn was shot
once in the chest with a nine
millimeter Browning handgun
shortly before 2 A.M.

Deborah Lewisohn heard
her mother say, "Jimmy,"
stop laying your trips
on me." Then a loud

report and glass
breaking. Then, "Jimmy,
call the hospital; I'm
bleeding." She asked
her father, "How could you

do this?" "Without love
and compassion," he
replied.

"I pulled the top of the
gun back, and it just
bolted forward. As I grabbed
hold of it, it went off."

Dinah Lewisohn came down
from her bedroom and saw
her father rise from a
kneeling position over
his wife. "If it'll make
you happy," he said,
"I'll shoot myself.
Then, at least, we'll
die together."

iii.

We entered with the women,
our hands already
broken from the scales.

Such sacrifice:
from two days' work
we carried the burden of numbers
within us.

Lifting the knife and
splitting them,
lopping off the heads

behind the gills,
our hands digging
for air sacks
so slimed became,
counting

(muscular bodies,
glazed, unseeing eyes)

"Do you know what I'd like to do?"
you said to me at lunch time over soup.

"I'd like to quit."

That night, I thought of it,
soaking in the tub. It seemed
the stench would never go away.

Nikko Shrine

The Shinto priest
gathers his robes
around him, proceeds
across the bridge
to the shrine.

You can hear his
wooden sandals
click against
the planks, pushing
snow in front

of him, catching
white and moisture
on his hem. He does
not stop to view
the mountains

rising like dreams
behind him or
the bright stream
rippling beneath—
how each seeks

completion in
the other, moving
toward purpose
beyond the pic-
ture's frame.

*

violent weather in the North
ice storms snow lines
of communication down

riotous winds uprooting
trees *Still*, she says, *we felt
safe in our houses…*

*

snow falls
lightly at first
then, more
insistently

cutting a path
across the win-
dow's square
white thick

white blinding
white the cold
breath from
human lungs
collecting

still
yet moving
the same
yet different
calm yet

not calm not
at all calm
but assuming
an air of
detachment

linked in this
slow dance

this dazzling
atmosphere

falling
somnambulant
apart

    *

The Buddhist bells
on my bedpost
ring softly as I
    sit down

warding off evil
spirits nightmares
uninvited reminders

of things left
undone loves
    lost
questioning

    *

Let no unhap-
    piness
come into this
    house

Awake at Midnight

                      I keep thinking
a phone will ring, but, then, I remember,
I have no phone, and if anyone were calling,
I could not hear them.
                      Last night, the moth
returned, throwing its fat body against
the glass. Tonight, behind the shade, it flaps
—flutter and thump—like a fish.
                            The sea
is making. I hear the periodic fury of assault.
No bell though, which means: this is just
the usual sea, dragging me from my dreams.

        ***

One man drowned, two men swelling
      in the sea, the rise and fall, the casual
hostility. This place contains multitudes. Do
they sleep in this raw weather?
                              Hear the rain
on the roof, the sea making; feel the damp
rise.

        ***

                    The moth spreads
its wings against the glass, peaceful at last;
my body yearns for sleep.

        ***

                    I dream of my
father in the frame of a boy, freckle-faced,
hair on end, leaning in to discover who this
might be. Startled to encounter
                          the familiar
across the divide

                    of time. MJ says,
"Bend your arm like this," and inserts
a needle there near the elbow. A flash
of energy rushes down through my arm

and out.
          "You are balanced. You have
energy. You just need more."

                 ***

                    And now,
human fatigue returns, a certain urge
for senselessness telling me:
                              fold body
beneath blankets and sleep. And I almost
fall for it, except
                    a bird begins to chirr,
as if it had seen something unusual,
as if something important were about
to happen.
          Hamlet's ghost fades. My
ghosts sleep on the hill, there where
the wind blows and, in a chorus of
breathlessness, doze, chilling themselves.

                 ***

                    This is a place
where consciousness rests—here, now,
brimming with possibility. Energy
gravitates, does not marvel, but accepts.

"Man does not know truth,
but embodies it." Woman also (that's me).
Whitman: "I contain multitudes."
               Gravitas.   The sea.

Coda

Yin Time

At Jan's   the animals come and go.

Ginger   the dachshund   who's been mixing it up with the neighbor's
labrador   taps down the hall   and over to me   expects
a long and thorough stroking.

I guide my hand along her back   Her eyes close contentedly.
When I'm done   she barks for more.

Her daughter's rescued cat (Haiku)   scratches to come in   circles   cries
for attention   We proceed with the treatment   Cat jumps on table
Jan takes her out   not hungry   missing something.

Usually hides in her daughter's room   afraid of the other cat
who crouches under the wicker chair   perfect camouflage.

Fountains bubble   giant goldfish pause   silken fans
in dark water flutter.

*

The presence of Chi in your hand: sensation of warmth   Do not attempt
to contain   but guide it.

I struggle to assume the postures   feel afterwards
energy coursing through me   old acupuncture points   lighting up like
lights on a switchboard.

Voices?
The sea was empty   Then the surge   filling the land   swelling
and drowning   (the emptiness

at the center: not so much a void as
a clearing of the slate).

*

Violent weather in the West   Snow in Maine   Here   it is
unseasonably warm: palm fronds sway

ever so slightly   Electric golf carts   glide serenely
along pathways   Blue skies silent   except for the occasional
jetliner easing down.

Cosam Rocking

Cosam is rocking on the front porch.
He does not speak, but wants me to know
he is grateful for the chance to feel
the breeze again, inhale the fresh air.

He sees the cows in the meadow, bending
to their meal, the freckled pond, the geese
on the surface paddling. He is not distracted
by the scratch of leaves, the thin chirr

of frogs, the vague and constant humming.
He sits upright in his chair, his ancient
fingers, opening. One day, he will tell me
what he is up to, reveal what he knows

and why he wants it said. But today he is
experiencing the pleasure of his toes,
the way the loose clay crumbles   free
when rocking. If the grave is a chance
to contemplate one's actions, then this
presence suggests a yearning for something
left undone. He will find a way to say it,
trust me. We will learn to speak again,
the truth.

Acknowledgements

Grateful acknowledgement is made to the following journals and anthologies in which some of these poems first appeared:

Barrow Street ("Phoenix")

Comstock Review ("Gargoyle," "Ghost Orchid")

Connecticut Review ("Mt. Pisgah")

Crazyhorse ("Acupuncture")

English Journal ("Mowing")

Louisiana Literature ("Chipola River")

Roanoke Review ("Nikko Shrine")

Saw Palm ("Cosam's Journey")

Superstition Review ("James Brown," "Awake at Midnight")

Trajectory ("Maine in Winter")

Watching the Perseids, Backwaters Press ("The Last Afternoon of My Father as Himself")

West Trade Review ("Norway," "Sturm und Drang," "Yin Time")

Willow Review ("Arabella in Covington")

Joann Gardner holds a master's degree in English from the University of York (England) and a PhD from The Johns Hopkins University. For thirty-nine years, she taught Literature and Creative Writing at Florida State University, during which time she co-founded, directed and taught for Runaway with Words, a poetry workshop for at-risk youth. She has held artist residencies at Villa Montalvo and The Blue Mountain Center, and is a member of the Community of Writers at Squaw Valley. Her critical and creative work has appeared nationally in a variety of books, journals and anthologies. Currently, she is working on two new poetry collections and is a frequent contributor of essays and reviews to *The Harpswell Anchor*.

www.ingramcontent.com/pod-product-compliance
Lightning Source LLC
Chambersburg PA
CBHW031126160426
43192CB00008B/1124